LARAVEL REST API
MADE EASY

LEARN TO WRITE FLUENT LARAVEL API

Omkar Panherkar

CONTENTS

TABLE OF CONTENTS

CHAPTER 1: INTRODUCTION TO LARAVEL AND RESTFUL API DESIGN

Good day! Welcome to the world of Laravel API development. We'll go over the fundamentals of the Laravel framework in this chapter and how it can be used to build killer RESTful APIs.

Taylor Otwell developed the well-known PHP framework Laravel in 2011.

It is renowned for having a clear syntax and strong capabilities that make it simple to build complex web applications with little code.

One of Laravel's strongest features is its built-in support for RESTful routing, which makes it simple to design routes that adhere to a RESTful API's rules.

Other amazing features of Laravel that make it ideal for developing APIs include support for various response formats, integrated pagination and sorting, versioning capabilities, rate limitation, and many more.

To build a RESTful API with Laravel, we need to define our routes using the appropriate HTTP methods, use controllers to handle requests and return appropriate responses, use models to interact with our database, implement authentication and authorization, and return the appropriate status codes and error messages.

In the next chapters, we'll dive deeper into each of these topics and give you examples to help you understand better. Let's get started!

CHAPTER 2: SETTING UP A LARAVEL DEVELOPMENT ENVIRONMENT

Alright, let's get our Laravel development environment set up! In this chapter, we'll cover what you need to have installed on your computer, how to create a new Laravel project and run it on a web server, and how to connect your project to a database.

Here's what you'll need before we start:

- **PHP 7.4 or later**
- **Composer**
- **A web server (Apache or Nginx)**
- **A database server (MySQL or PostgreSQL)**

Once you have all that squared away, use Composer to create a new Laravel project by running this command in your terminal:

```
composer create-project --prefer-dist laravel/laravel your-project-name
```

This will create a new Laravel project in a directory called "your-project-name". Navigate into that directory and run **"php artisan serve"** to start the built-in development server and make your application available at http://localhost:8000.

Next, we'll set up the database connection by editing the .env file in the root of your project. You'll need to set the following variables in the .env file:

DB_CONNECTION: The type of database you are using (mysql, sqlite, etc.)

DB_HOST: The hostname of your database server

DB_PORT: The port number of your database server

DB_DATABASE: The name of your database

DB_USERNAME: The username used to connect to your database

DB_PASSWORD: The password used to connect to your database

Once that's done, use the php artisan migrate command to create the tables in your database, and if you have sample data, you can use the php artisan db:seed command to seed it.

And that's it! You're all set up and ready to start building your Laravel application. In the next chapter, we'll dive into routing and controllers, which are essential for building a RESTful API with Laravel.

CHAPTER 3: ROUTING AND CONTROLLERS IN LARAVEL FOR API DESIGN

In this chapter, we'll talk about routing and controllers in Laravel, and how they play an important role in building a RESTful API.

Routing in Laravel

Routing in Laravel is used to define the URLs that a user can visit and the actions that should be taken when those URLs are accessed. In a RESTful API, routes are used to map the URL to the appropriate controller function.

In Laravel, you can define your routes in the routes/web.php or routes/api.php file. The web.php file is used for web routes and the api.php file is used for API routes.

To define a route, you can use the Route facade and specify the HTTP method, the URL, and the controller action that should be called when the URL is accessed. For example, to create a route for a GET request to /users, you can use the following code:

```
Route::get('/users', 'UserController@index');
```

This will call the index method on the UserController class when a GET request is made to the /users URL.

In addition to the basic routing, Laravel also provides a number of other routing features that are useful for API development, such as:

Route parameters: Allows you to capture values from the URL and pass them to the controller function

Named routes: Allows you to give a name to a route, making it easier to generate URLs in your views or controllers

Group routing: Allows you to group routes together and apply middleware or namespaces to them

Controllers in Laravel are used to handle requests

Let's talk more about controllers! So, controllers in Laravel act like the boss of the route. They handle the logic of your application and make sure the right response is sent back to the user. Think of them as the traffic cop directing the flow of data.

Each controller method (also known as actions) corresponds to a specific route and is responsible for performing specific tasks.

For example, you could have a UserController with actions like index, store, update, and destroy.

The index action would handle the route for fetching all the users, the store action would handle the route for creating a new user, the update action would handle the route for updating an existing user, and the destroy action would handle the route for deleting a user.

In addition, controllers can also use middleware to protect certain routes and methods from unauthorized access.

This means you can use middleware to authenticate a user before allowing them to access certain routes or actions.

In short, controllers are like the boss of the route, they handle the logic of your application and make sure the right response is sent back to the user, They also have the capability to use middleware to protect certain routes and methods from unauthorized access.

Sure, let's talk about how to make controllers in Laravel!

To create a new controller, you can use the Artisan command-line interface. For example, to create a new controller called UserController, you can run the following command:

```
php artisan make:controller UserController
```

This will create a new file in the app/Http/Controllers directory called UserController.php. You can then add methods (also known as actions) to the controller that correspond to different routes.

It's important to note that in Laravel, controllers should be used for handling the logic of your application and returning a response, not for handling the presentation of data to the user. This is the job of views.

You can also use the --resource option when creating a controller to create a controller with methods for all the RESTful actions, like this:

```
php artisan make:controller UserController --resource
```

This command will create a new UserController with methods for index, create, store, show, edit, update, and destroy actions.

You can also use the --model option to generate a controller that is already bound to a specific model:

```
php artisan make:controller UserController --model=User
```

In short, creating a new controller in Laravel is easy and can be done using the Artisan command-line interface

CHAPTER 4. CREATING AND MANAGING DATABASE MODELS IN LARAVEL

Creating and managing database models in Laravel is a breeze, thanks to the powerful Eloquent ORM (Object-Relational Mapping) included in the framework. In this chapter, we'll go over the basics of creating and working with models in Laravel, as well as some of the more advanced features that Eloquent provides.

First, let's start by creating a new model. In Laravel, models are typically stored in the "app" directory. To create a new model, you can use the built-in command-line tool "Artisan" by running the following command:

```
php artisan make:model ModelName
```

This will create a new file in the "app" directory called "ModelName.php". By default, the model will be empty, but you can add methods and properties to it as needed.

Next, let's take a look at how to connect a model to a database table. In order to do this, you'll need to specify the name of the table that the model should be connected to, as well as any other details that are required to connect to the database.

Copy code

```php
<?php
class ModelName extends Model
{
    protected $table = 'table_name';
}
```

This is the basic setup needed to connect a model to a database table, now you can start querying the table by calling the model.

```
$users = ModelName::all();
```

Eloquent makes it easy to work with your database records using an object-oriented syntax. You can retrieve all records from a table using the "all" method, or retrieve a single record using the "find" method. You can also use various other methods to retrieve records based on different criteria, such as the "where" method, the "orderBy" method, and the "groupBy" method.

Once you've retrieved your records, you can work with them just like you would with any other object. You can access properties, call methods, and even save changes back to the database.

Copy code

```
$user = ModelName::find(1); $user->name = 'John Doe'; $user->save();
```

You can also use the create method to insert new records into the database.

```
ModelName::create(['name' => 'Jane Doe', 'email' => 'jane@example.com']);
```

Another important feature of Eloquent is the ability to define relationships between models. For example, if you have a "users" table and a "posts" table, you can define a relationship between the two so that you can easily retrieve all of the posts for a particular user.

```php
<?php
class User extends Model
{
    public function posts()
    {
        return $this->hasMany(Post::class);
    }
}
class Post extends Model
{
    public function user()
    {
        return $this->belongsTo(User::class);
    }
}
```

You can easily retrieve the posts for a user by calling the "posts" method on the user object, like so:

```
$user = User::find(1); $posts = $user->posts;
```

In conclusion, Laravel's Eloquent ORM is a powerful tool that makes it easy to work with your database models. It provides a simple, intuitive syntax for creating, retrieving, and manipulating records in your database, as well as powerful features like relationships and model events. Additionally, it offers advanced features like eager loading, which allows you to retrieve related records in a single query, thus reducing the number of queries needed to retrieve all the data.

Another important feature to mention is the ability to define custom primary keys, which is useful if you're working with legacy databases with non-integer primary keys.

It's also worth noting that Eloquent supports multiple database systems, including MySQL, PostgreSQL, SQLite, and more. This makes it a great choice for projects that need to work with different database systems.

In summary, Laravel's Eloquent ORM makes working with databases in Laravel easy, intuitive and efficient, with its simple syntax and powerful features, it's a great choice for web developers looking for a robust and flexible database solution.

CHAPTER 5. HANDLING API REQUESTS AND RESPONSES IN LARAVEL

Handling API requests and responses in Laravel is a breeze, thanks to the built-in support for RESTful controllers and API resources. In this chapter, we'll go over the basics of handling API requests and responses in Laravel, as well as some of the more advanced features that the framework provides.

First, let's start by creating a new API route. In Laravel, you can define API routes just like you would with any other route, but with a few extra options to specify that it's an API route.

Copy code

Route::apiResource('/users', 'UserController');

This will create routes for index, show, store, update, and delete methods.

Now, let's create a new controller for handling API requests. In Laravel, controllers are typically stored in the "app/Http/Controllers" directory. To create a new controller, you can use the built-in command-line tool "Artisan" by running the following command:

```
php artisan make:controller UserController --api
```

This will create a new file in the "app/Http/Controllers" directory called "UserController.php", with all the necessary methods for handling API requests, such as index, show, store, update, and delete.

Next, let's take a look at how to handle API requests in the controller. In order to handle API requests, you'll need to define methods for each type of request. For example, the "index" method will handle a request to retrieve a list of all users, while the "show" method will handle a request to retrieve a single user.

```php
<?php
class UserController extends Controller
{
    public function index()
    {
        $users = User::all();
        return response()->json($users);
    }
    public function show($id)
    {
        $user = User::find($id);
        return response()->json($user);
    }
}
```

In the example above, we're using the "response" helper to create a JSON response containing the users data, which we then return to the client.

Another important feature of Laravel's API support is the ability to use API Resources. API Resources are classes that transform your models into a JSON representation suitable for API responses.

```php
<?php
class UserResource extends JsonResource
{
    public function toArray($request)
    {
        return ['id' => $this->id, 'name' => $this->name, 'email' => $this->email,];
    }
}
```

```php
<?php
class UserController extends Controller
{
    public function show($id)
    {
        $user = User::find($id);
        return new UserResource($user);
    }
}
```

In this example, we've created a UserResource class that transforms a User model into a JSON representation that includes the user's ID, name, and email address. We can then use this resource in our controller to return a JSON response containing the user's data.

Another feature worth mentioning is the validation feature Laravel provides, which allows you to validate incoming requests before they are processed.

```php
<?php
class UserController extends Controller {
  public function store(Request $request) {
    $validatedData = $request->validate([
      'name' => 'required|max:255',
      'email' => 'required|email|unique:users',
      'password' => 'required|min:6' ]);
    User::create($validatedData);
    return response()->json(['message' => 'User created successfully']);
  }
}
```

In the example above, we're using the "validate" method on the incoming request object to check that the request contains a valid name, email, and password. If the validation fails, an exception will be thrown and the user will be returned an error message.

In addition to these features, Laravel also provides support for handling API authentication and authorization. You can use Laravel's built-in authentication features to protect your API routes and ensure that only authorized users can access them.

In conclusion, Laravel's support for handling API requests and responses makes it easy to create powerful and flexible APIs. Its built-in support for RESTful controllers, API resources, and validation make it simple to handle incoming requests and return appropriate responses. Additionally, the framework's support for authentication and authorization allows you to secure your APIs and ensure that only authorized users can access them. With all these features, Laravel is a great choice for developers looking to create robust and secure APIs for their projects.

CHAPTER 6. IMPLEMENTING API AUTHENTICATION AND AUTHORIZATION IN LARAVEL

Implementing API authentication and authorization in Laravel is a straightforward process, thanks to the built-in support for authentication and authorization in the framework. In this chapter, we'll go over the basics of implementing API authentication and authorization in Laravel, as well as some of the more advanced features that the framework provides.

First, let's start by configuring authentication for our API. In Laravel, you can use the built-in "Auth" facade to configure authentication for your API. To do this, you'll need to specify the guard that should be used for authentication, as well as the provider that should be used to retrieve the user's credentials.

Copy code

```
'guards' => [
    'web' => [ 'driver' => 'session', 'provider' => 'users', ],
    'api' => [ 'driver' => 'token', 'provider' => 'users', 'hash' => false, ],
]
```

In the example above, we're configuring the "api" guard to use the "token" driver and the "users" provider. This means that when a client makes a request to our API, it should include an authentication token in the request headers, and we'll use the "users" provider to look up the user's credentials based on that token.

Next, let's take a look at how to handle API requests that require authentication. In Laravel, you can use the "auth" middleware to protect routes that should only be accessible by authenticated users.

```php
<?php
Route::middleware(['auth:api'])->group(function () {
    Route::get('/users', 'UserController@index');
    Route::get('/users/{id}', 'UserController@show');
});
```

In the example above, we're using the "auth:api" middleware to protect the "users" and "users/{id}" routes. This means that when a client makes a request to one of these routes, it will first be checked to see if the client has included a valid authentication token in the request headers. If a valid token is not found, the client will receive a "401 Unauthorized" response.

Once we have authentication set up, we can move on to authorization. Laravel provides a simple and elegant way to authorize user actions by using policies. Policies are classes that determine if a user is authorized to perform a certain action on a certain resource.

```php
<?php
class UserPolicy
{
    public function update(User $user, User $model)
    {
        return $user->id === $model->id;
    }
}
```

```php
<?php
class UserController extends Controller
{
    public function update(Request $request, User $user)
    {
        $this->authorize('update', $user);
        // update user logic
    }
}
```

In this example, we've created a "UserPolicy" class with an "update" method that checks if the authenticated user's ID matches the ID of the user they're trying to update. We can then use the "authorize" method in our controller to check if the user is authorized to update the user. If the user is not authorized, an exception will be thrown, and the user will be returned an error message.

Additionally, Laravel also provides support for role-based authentication and authorization. You can use Laravel's built-in "Gate" facade to define roles

and assign them to users, and then use those roles to determine if a user is authorized to perform a certain action.

```php
<?php
class User
{
  public function roles()
  {
    return $this->belongsToMany(Role::class);
  }
}
```

```php
<?php
class UserController extends Controller
{

  public function update(Request $request, User $user)
  {

    if ($user->hasRole('admin')) {
      // update user logic
    } else {
      return response()->json(['message' => 'Unauthorized'], 403);
    }

  }

}
```

In the above example, we've defined a many-to-many relationship between the User and Role models, allowing a user to have multiple roles. We can then use the "hasRole" method on the user object to check if the user has a specific role, in this case, an "admin" role.

In conclusion, Laravel provides a solid and flexible solution for implementing API authentication and authorization. Its built-in support for guards, middleware, policies, and gates makes it easy to secure your API routes and ensure that only authorized users can access them. Additionally, the framework's support for role-based authentication and authorization allows you to control user access at a more granular level. With all these features, Laravel is a great choice for developers looking to create secure and well-controlled APIs for their projects.

CHAPTER 7.ERROR HANDLING AND DEBUGGING IN LARAVEL API DEVELOPMENT

Error handling and debugging in Laravel API development is an important aspect to consider when building a robust and reliable API. In this chapter, we'll go over the basics of error handling and debugging in Laravel, as well as some of the more advanced features that the framework provides.

First, let's start by configuring error handling for our API. In Laravel, you can use the built-in "**config/app.php**" file to configure error handling for your API.

Copy code

```
'debug' => env('APP_DEBUG', false),
```

In the above example, we're setting the "debug" value to false, which means that Laravel will not show any detailed error messages in production. However, you can set it to true for development environment, to see detailed error messages which can be helpful during debugging.

Next, let's take a look at how to handle exceptions in our API. In Laravel, you can use the built-in "app/Exceptions/Handler.php" file to handle exceptions and return appropriate responses to the client.

```php
<?php
class Handler extends ExceptionHandler
{
  public function render($request, Exception $exception)
  {
    if ($exception instanceof ValidationException) {
        return response()->json(['error' => $exception->validator->errors(),],
$exception->status);
    }
```

```
    return parent::render($request, $exception);
  }
}
```

In the example above, we're checking if the exception thrown is a ValidationException and returning a JSON response with the error messages and appropriate status code to the client.

Another important aspect of error handling in Laravel is logging. Laravel provides a built-in logging system that allows you to log errors and exceptions to various storage options such as files, databases, and even cloud services like AWS.

Copy code

```
Log::error('An error occurred', ['context' => $exception]);
```

In the example above, we're using the "error" method of the "Log" facade to log an error message along with the exception context, which can be very helpful in debugging.

Another important feature worth mentioning is the ability to create custom error pages in Laravel. You can create custom views for different error types and return them to the client.

Copy code

```php
<?php
class Handler extends ExceptionHandler
{
  public function render($request, Exception $exception)
  {
    if ($exception instanceof NotFoundHttpException) {
      return response()->view('errors.404', [], 404);
    }
    return parent::render($request, $exception);
  }
}
```

In this example, we're checking if the exception thrown is a NotFoundHttpException and returning a custom view "errors.404" with a 404 status code to the client.

In conclusion, error handling and debugging in Laravel API development is an important aspect to consider when building a robust and reliable API. Laravel provides a built-in error handling and logging system that makes it easy to handle exceptions and log errors. Additionally, the framework's support for custom error pages allows you to return appropriate responses to the client in case of errors. With all these features, Laravel is a great choice for developers looking to create error-free and reliable APIs for their projects.

CHAPTER 8. OPTIMIZING AND SCALING LARAVEL APIS

Optimizing and scaling Laravel APIs can be a bit tricky, but with the right techniques and tools, it can be done with ease. In this chapter, we'll be diving into some key concepts and strategies for optimizing and scaling your Laravel-based APIs.

First, let's talk about performance optimization. One of the most important things to keep in mind when optimizing the performance of your API is to keep your routes lean and mean. This means minimizing the number of routes you have and reducing the complexity of each route. This can be done by using route caching, which will speed up the processing of your routes by caching them in memory. Additionally, you should try to limit the number of middleware that are applied to each route, as these can also add unnecessary overhead.

Another important factor to consider when optimizing the performance of your API is to minimize the number of database queries that are being executed. This can be done by using eager loading, which loads the associated data for a model in a single query, rather than multiple queries. Additionally, you should try to minimize the number of joins that are being used in your queries, as these can also add unnecessary overhead.

Now let's talk about scaling. When it comes to scaling your API, there are several different strategies that you can use. One popular strategy is to use a load balancer, which will distribute incoming requests across multiple servers, thus reducing the load on a single server. Additionally, you can also use caching to reduce the load on your database and improve the performance of your API.

Another strategy for scaling your API is to use horizontal scaling, which involves adding more servers to your infrastructure as your user base grows. This can be done by using a service like Amazon Web Services (AWS) or Google Cloud Platform (GCP), which allow you to easily add more servers to your infrastructure as needed.

Last but not least, don't forget to monitor your API performance and usage metrics. This will help you identify areas where you need to optimize and scale your API, and will give you a better understanding of how your users are interacting with your API.

In summary, optimizing and scaling Laravel APIs requires a combination of techniques and tools like performance optimization, caching, load balancer, horizontal scaling and monitoring of performance and usage metrics. By keeping your routes lean and mean, minimizing database queries and adding more servers to your infrastructure as needed, you can ensure that your API can handle a growing user base and provide a smooth experience for your users.

CHAPTER 9.DEPLOYMENT AND TESTING OF LARAVEL APIS

Deployment and testing of Laravel APIs is an important aspect to consider when building and launching a production-ready API. In this chapter, we'll go over the basics of deploying and testing Laravel APIs, as well as some of the more advanced features that the framework provides.

First, let's start by discussing deployment. In Laravel, you can use a variety of methods to deploy your API, including using a traditional web server like Apache or Nginx, or using a cloud-based service like AWS Elastic Beanstalk or Heroku.

One popular method for deploying Laravel APIs is using a tool like Forge, which automates the process of setting up and deploying a Laravel application on a server. Forge also provides additional features such as server monitoring, database management, and easy SSL certificate installation.

Another popular method is using a platform-as-a-service (PaaS) like Heroku, which allows you to easily deploy your Laravel application with a few simple commands. Heroku also provides additional features such as automatic scaling, add-ons for various services like databases, and easy integration with other tools like GitHub and CircleCI.

Once your API is deployed, it's important to test it thoroughly to ensure that it's working as expected and that there are no bugs or issues. In Laravel, you can use a variety of testing tools, including the built-in PHPUnit testing framework, as well as tools like Behat for behavior-driven development (BDD) testing.

PHPUnit allows you to write unit tests for your application to ensure that individual components are working correctly.

```php
<?php
class UserTest extends TestCase
{

  public function testCreateUser()
  {
            $user = new User(['name' => 'John Doe', 'email' =>
'johndoe@example.com', 'password' => bcrypt('secret'),]);
    $this->assertTrue($user->save());

  }

}
```

In the example above, we're creating a new user, and then asserting that it is saved successfully.

Behat, on the other hand, allows you to write tests that describe the behavior of your application from the user's perspective.

Copy code

Feature: User registration In order to use the application As a user I need to be able to register Scenario: Successful registration Given I am on the registration page When I fill in the registration form with valid data And I submit the form Then I should see a confirmation message

In the example above, we're describing the behavior of a user registering on the application, including the steps they take and the outcome they should expect.

Laravel also provides support for API testing by allowing you to send HTTP requests to your application and examine the responses. This feature allows you to test your API endpoints and ensure that they are working correctly.

Copy code

```php
<?php
class UserTest extends TestCase
{

  public function testGetUsers()
  {
    $response = $this->get('/api/users');
```

```
$response->assertStatus(200);
    }
}
```

In this example, we're sending a GET request to the "/api/users" endpoint and asserting that the response has a status code of 200, indicating that the request was successful.

In conclusion, deploying and testing Laravel APIs is an important aspect to consider when building and launching a production-ready API. Laravel provides a variety of methods for deploying your API,

including traditional web servers, cloud-based services, and automation tools. Additionally, the framework provides a variety of testing tools, including PHPUnit and Behat for unit and behavioral testing, and built-in support for API testing, which makes it easy to ensure that your API is working as expected and that there are no bugs or issues. With all these features, Laravel is a great choice for developers looking to create and launch high-quality and reliable APIs for their projects. It's important to remember that testing and deployment is an ongoing process and it's important to continually monitor, test and update the API to ensure it's running smoothly and securely.

Another important aspect of deploying and testing your Laravel API is security. It's essential to ensure that your API is secure against common threats like SQL injection, cross-site scripting (XSS), and cross-site request forgery (CSRF). Laravel provides built-in protection against these threats, but it's important to continually monitor and test your API to ensure that it's secure.

Another aspect to consider is load testing, which is the process of putting your API under heavy load and measuring its performance. This is important to ensure that your API can handle the expected amount of traffic and that it can scale effectively as the traffic increases. Laravel provides support for load testing via tools like Apache JMeter, which can help you simulate heavy loads and test the performance of your API.

Lastly, after you've deployed your API, it's important to monitor it for any issues or errors. Laravel provides support for monitoring via tools like Bugsnag, which can help you track and fix errors and crashes in your API. Additionally, monitoring your API's performance and user engagement can help you understand how your API is being used and identify areas for improvement.

In conclusion, deploying and testing Laravel APIs is an important aspect to consider when building and launching a production-ready API. Laravel provides a variety of methods for deploying your API, as well as built-in support for testing and security. However, it's important to remember that deployment and testing is an ongoing process and it's essential to continually monitor, test, and update your API to ensure it's running smoothly and securely. With all these features, Laravel is a great choice for developers looking to create and launch high-quality and reliable APIs for their projects.

CHAPTER 10. ADVANCED TOPICS IN LARAVEL API DEVELOPMENT SUCH AS CACHING AND EVENT HANDLING

As your Laravel API grows and evolves, you may find that you need to implement more advanced features to optimize performance, improve scalability, and add new functionality. In this chapter, we'll discuss two advanced topics in Laravel API development: caching and event handling.

First, let's talk about caching. Caching is a technique that allows you to store frequently-used data in memory, so that it can be quickly retrieved without having to go back to the database or other data source. This can significantly improve the performance of your API, especially if you have a lot of read-heavy operations.

Laravel provides built-in support for caching, making it easy to add caching to your API. One popular method for caching in Laravel is using the built-in "Cache" facade.

```php
<?php
use Illuminate\Support\Facades\Cache;
class UserController extends Controller
{
  public function index()
  {
    $users = Cache::remember('users', 60, function () {
      return User::all(); });
    return $users;
  }
}
```

In the example above, we're using the "remember" method of the "Cache" facade to cache the result of the "User::all()" query for 60 minutes. This means that if the same request is made within 60 minutes, the cached result will be returned, rather than querying the database again.

Another advanced topic in Laravel API development is event handling. Events are a way to send notifications or trigger actions when certain events occur in your application. This allows you to decouple different parts of your application, making it more modular and easier to maintain.

Laravel provides built-in support for events, making it easy to add event handling to your API. You can use the built-in "Event" facade to trigger events, and the "EventServiceProvider" to listen for events and register event handlers.

Copy code

```
Event::listen('user.registered', function ($user) {
  // send welcome email
});
```

In the example above, we're using the "listen" method of the "Event" facade to listen for the "**user.registered**" event, and then we're registering a closure to be executed when that event is triggered. This closure could be used to send a welcome email to the user when they register.

You can also use the "EventServiceProvider" to register event handlers for your application.

Copy code

```
<?php
class EventServiceProvider extends ServiceProvider
{
  protected $listen = [
    UserRegistered::class => [
      SendWelcomeEmail::class,
      NotifyAdmin::class,
    ],
  ];
}
```

In the example above, we're registering multiple event handlers for the "**UserRegistered**" event, these handlers are the classes "**SendWelcomeEmail**" and "**NotifyAdmin**" which will be executed when the event is triggered.

In conclusion, caching and event handling are advanced topics in Laravel API development that can help you optimize performance, improve scalability, and add new functionality to your API. Laravel provides built-in support for both caching and event handling, making it easy to add these features to your API. Caching can help you improve the performance of your API by storing frequently-used data in memory, while event handling allows you to decouple different parts of your application and add new functionality easily. With all these features, Laravel is a great choice for developers looking to create advanced and scalable APIs for their projects.

CHAPTER 11. CREATE TODO APP API

Creating a Todo API sample in Laravel is a great way to learn how to build a simple but functional API using the framework. In this chapter, we'll go through the process of creating a Todo API that allows users to create, read, update, and delete tasks.

First, let's start by creating the necessary models and migrations for our Todo API. In Laravel, you can use the built-in command line tools to generate models and migrations.

php artisan make:model Todo -m

This command will generate a new model called "Todo" and a corresponding migration file. The migration file will be used to create the "todos" table in the database with the following fields: "id", "task", "completed", "created_at" and "updated_at".

Next, we'll need to create the necessary controllers for our Todo API. In Laravel, you can use the built-in command line tools to generate controllers.

php artisan make:controller TodoController

This command will generate a new controller called "TodoController" which we'll use to handle all the HTTP requests for our Todo API.

Now that we have our models, migrations, and controllers set up, we can start adding the necessary routes for our Todo API. In Laravel, you can define routes in the "routes/web.php" or "routes/api.php" file, depending on whether you're building a web or API application.

Copy code

```
Route::apiResource('todos', 'TodoController');
```

This line of code will register routes for the standard RESTful actions (index, store, show, update, and delete) for the Todo resource.

With our routes set up, we can now start implementing the logic for our Todo API in the TodoController. In the controller, we'll define methods for each of the standard RESTful actions, such as index, store, show, update, and delete.

Copy code

```php
<?php
class TodoController extends Controller
{
  public function index()
  {
    return Todo::all();
  }
  public function store(Request $request)
  {
    $todo = Todo::create($request->all());
    return response()->json($todo, 201);
  }
  public function show($id)
  {
    $todo = Todo::findOrFail($id);
    return $todo;
  }
  public function update(Request $request, $id)
  {
    $todo = Todo::findOrFail($id);
    $todo->update($request->all());
    return $todo;
  }
  public function delete($id)
  {
    $todo = Todo::findOrFail($id);
    $todo->delete();
    return response()->json(null, 204);
  }
}
```

In the example above, we've defined methods for each of the standard RESTful actions. The "index" method returns all the todos, the "store" method creates a new todo, the "show" method returns a specific todo by id, the "update" method updates an existing todo, and the "delete" method deletes a todo. With our Todo API fully implemented, we can now test it using a tool like Postman to send HTTP requests to our API and check the responses. You can test the different routes and see the results. In conclusion, creating a Todo API sample in Laravel is a great way to learn how to build a simple but functional API using the framework. Laravel provides built-in support for models, migrations, controllers, and routing, making it easy to set up and implement a Todo API. Additionally, the framework's support for RESTful actions allows you to easily handle the standard CRUD operations for your Todo resource. With all these features, Laravel is a great choice for developers looking to create a simple and functional Todo API for their projects.

CHAPTER 12. UPLOADING LARAVEL API MICROSERVICE ON GOOGLE CLOUD

Uploading a Laravel-based API microservice to a Ubuntu VM on Google Cloud using Apache can seem like a daunting task, but with the right tools and strategies, it can be done with ease. In this chapter, we'll be diving into the process of uploading your Laravel API microservice to a Ubuntu VM on Google Cloud using Apache, highlighting some important points along the way.

Prepare your Laravel API microservice for deployment:

One of the most important things to keep in mind when deploying your API is to make sure that it is properly configured for production. This means setting the appropriate environment variables, such as the database connection settings, as well as disabling debugging and error reporting.

APP_ENV=production

APP_DEBUG=false

Another important step is to optimize your application for performance. This can be done by enabling caching and minifying your assets, as well as by using a service like Cloudflare to handle the delivery of your assets.

php artisan config:cache php artisan route:cache php artisan view:cache

Create a Google Cloud account:

Once your Laravel API microservice is prepared for deployment, the next step is to create a Google Cloud account. Once you've created an account, you'll need to create a new project, where you'll be able to deploy your API.

Set up a Ubuntu VM on Google Cloud:

Next, you'll need to set up a Ubuntu VM on Google Cloud. This can be done by using the Google Cloud Console, where you'll be able to select the appropriate machine type, operating system, and other settings for your VM. Once your VM is set up, you'll need to connect to it using SSH.

gcloud compute ssh my-vm-1 --project my-project-id --zone us-central1-a

Install Apache and PHP on Ubuntu:

With your VM set up and connected, the next step is to install Apache and PHP on the Ubuntu VM. This can be done by using the apt package manager.

sudo apt update sudo apt install apache2 sudo apt install php libapache2-mod-php php-mysql

Deploy your API:

Once Apache and PHP are installed, you can deploy your API by copying the files from your local machine to the VM. You can use the scp command to copy the files from your local machine to the VM.

scp -r /path/to/local/app/ root@my-vm-1:/var/www/app

Configure Apache to handle incoming requests:

After your API has been deployed, the final step is to configure Apache to handle incoming requests to your API. This can be done by creating a virtual host for your application.

sudo nano /etc/apache2/sites-available/app.conf

```
<VirtualHost *:80>
    ServerName example.com
    DocumentRoot /var/www/app/public
  <Directory /var/www/app/public>
      AllowOverride All Require all granted
  </Directory>
</VirtualHost>
```

sudo a2ensite app.conf

sudo service apache2 reload

In summary, uploading a Laravel API microservice to a Ubuntu VM on Google Cloud using Apache requires you to prepare your API for production by setting the appropriate environment variables, optimize the performance of your API by enabling caching and minifying assets, creating a Google Cloud account, setting up a Ubuntu VM, installing Apache and PHP, deploying your API and configuring Apache to handle incoming requests. With the right tools and strategies, you can ensure that your API is properly deployed and configured to handle incoming requests and provide a smooth experience for your users.

It's important to note that, during this process, you should also consider the security of your API, such as securing your server with a firewall, and making sure that all the components of your API are up to date. Also, you can implement an autoscaling mechanism to make sure that your API can handle an increase in traffic.

Additionally, it's important to monitor and maintain your API on regular basis to ensure that it's running smoothly and to address any issues that may arise.

With this, you have successfully uploaded your Laravel API microservice on a Ubuntu VM on Google Cloud using Apache, and it's ready to handle incoming requests and provide a smooth experience for your users.

CHAPTER 13.WHAT IS TOKEN BASED AUTHENTICATION & OAUTH2.0

When it comes to authenticating users in a web application, one of the most popular approaches is token-based authentication. Token-based authentication is a method of securely transmitting information between parties, through a token which is generated by one party and can be verified by another. In this chapter, we'll be diving into the concept of token-based authentication, specifically in the context of the Laravel PHP framework, and give you some examples of code.

First, let's talk about what token-based authentication is and how it works. In token-based authentication, a user is required to provide their credentials (e.g. email and password) to the application, which then sends a request to the server to authenticate the user. If the user is successfully authenticated, the server generates a token and sends it back to the user. This token is then sent with every subsequent request to the server, and is used to verify the user's identity and authorize access to the application's resources.

For example, here is a sample code of how you can use token-based authentication in Laravel

Copy code

```php
<?php
class LoginController extends Controller
{
  public function login(Request $request)
  {
    $credentials = $request->only('email', 'password');
    if (Auth::attempt($credentials)) {
      $token = Auth::user()->createToken('Access Token')->accessToken;
      return response()->json(['token' => $token], 200);
```

```
    } else {
        return response()->json(['error' => 'Unauthorized'], 401);
    }
}
```

This code uses the Auth facade to attempt to authenticate the user with the provided email and password, and if successful, it creates a token for the user using the createToken method provided by Laravel's built-in TokenGuard class. The accessToken property of the returned token can then be used to authenticate the user on subsequent requests.

Now, let's talk about OAuth2.0, which is an open-standard for authorization. OAuth2.0 is a widely adopted standard for token-based authentication, and is supported by many popular web services and social media platforms. In OAuth2.0, a user's credentials are used to request an access token from an authorization server, which can then be used to access the user's resources on a resource server.

In Laravel, token-based authentication and OAuth2.0 can be implemented using the built-in auth scaffolding, which provides a simple and easy-to-use interface for handling user authentication and authorization. Additionally, Laravel also provides a built-in Passport library, which is a simple, easy-to-use OAuth2.0 server implementation. Passport makes it easy to implement token-based authentication for your application, and also provides a simple and intuitive interface for managing and revoking access tokens.

For example, here is a sample code of how you can use OAuth2.0 in Laravel using the Passport library

```php
<?php
use Laravel\Passport\Passport;
class AuthController extends Controller
{
    public function __construct()
```

```
{
    Passport::routes();
}
public function login(Request $request)
{
        $credentials = ['email' => $request->email, 'password' => $request->password];
    if (
        Auth::attempt($credentials)
    ) {
        $user = Auth::user();
        $token = $user->createToken('Access Token')->accessToken;
        return response()->json(['token' => $token, 'user' => $user], 200);
    } else {
        return response()->json(['error' => 'Unauthorized'], 401);
    }
}
}
```

This code uses the `Passport` facade to create the necessary routes for handling OAuth2.0 requests, such as `/oauth/token` for generating access tokens. The `createToken` method is used to generate an access token for the authenticated user, which can then be used to access the user's resources on the resource server. In summary, token-based authentication is a secure method of authenticating users in a web application, which allows for a more decoupled authentication process. OAuth2.0 is a widely adopted standard for token-based authentication, and is supported by many popular web services and social media platforms. Laravel provides built-in support for token-based authentication and OAuth2.0, through the auth scaffolding and Passport library, which makes it easy to implement token-based authentication for your application. The example provided are just a sample of how you can use token-based authentication and OAuth2.0 in Laravel, and you can customize it according to your need.

CHAPTER 14.USING PASSPORT PACKAGE IN LARAVEL EMPLOYEE APP FOR OAUTH2.0

When it comes to building a robust and secure authentication system for an employee app, using the Passport package in Laravel is a great choice. Passport is an OAuth2.0 server implementation built specifically for Laravel and makes it simple to handle token-based authentication for your application. In this chapter, we'll be diving into the process of setting up and using Passport in a Laravel-based employee app, highlighting some important points along the way.

Here are some key points to keep in mind when using Passport for OAuth2.0 in a Laravel employee app:

Passport provides built-in support for token-based authentication and OAuth2.0, which makes it easy to handle user authentication and authorization.

Passport is easy to set up and use, and provides a simple and intuitive interface for managing and revoking access tokens.

Passport offers a simple and easy-to-use OAuth2.0 server implementation that can be integrated into your employee app, allowing you to provide a secure and robust authentication system for your employees.

Passport allows you to generate various types of tokens, such as personal access tokens, and also provides the ability to revoke them.

Passport also provides built-in support for handling OAuth2.0 clients and scopes, making it easy to define the permissions of your employees and control the access of your app's resources.

Here is an example of how you can use the Passport package in a Laravel-based employee app:

composer require laravel/passport

This command installs the Passport package and its dependencies.

php artisan migrate

This command creates the necessary database tables for storing clients and access tokens.

php artisan passport:install

This command creates the encryption keys needed to generate access tokens, as well as the personal access and password grant client.

```php
<?php
class EmployeeController extends Controller
{

  public function __construct()
  {

    $this->middleware('auth:api');

  }
  public function index()

  {

    $employees = Employee::all();
    return response()->json($employees);

  }

}
```

This code uses the `auth:api` middleware provided by Passport to protect the `index` method of the `EmployeeController`, ensuring that only authenticated users can access the employee data.

```php
<?php
class AuthController extends Controller
{

  public function login(Request $request)
  {

      $credentials = ['email' => $request->email, 'password' => $request->password];
    if (Auth::attempt($credentials)) {
      $user = Auth::user();
      $token = $user->createToken('Access Token')->accessToken;
      return response()->json(['token' => $token, 'user' => $user], 200);
    } else {
      return response()->json(['error' => 'Unauthorized'], 401);

    }

  }

}
```

This code uses the `Auth` facade to authenticate the user with the provided email and password, and if successful, it creates an access token for the user using the `createToken` method provided by Passport. The `accessToken` property of the returned token can then be used to authenticate the user on subsequent requests. In summary, Passport is a great choice when building a robust and secure authentication system for an employee app using Laravel. It is easy to set up and use, provides a simple and intuitive interface for managing and revoking access tokens, allows you to generate various types of tokens and offers built-in support for handling OAuth2.0 clients and scopes. By following these simple steps and examples, you will be able to implement Passport in your employee app, providing a secure and reliable authentication system for your employees.

CHAPTER 15.IS USING API RESOURCES IN LARAVEL GOOD OR BAD?

When it comes to building APIs in Laravel, one of the most popular choices is to use API resources. API resources are a way to represent and transform your models into a format that is easily consumable by your clients. They provide a simple and easy-to-use interface for handling data transformations and can be a great tool for building APIs. But like anything, there are pros and cons to using API resources, so let's dive in and explore them.

First, let's talk about the pros of using API resources in Laravel:

API resources provide a simple and easy-to-use interface for handling data transformations. They allow you to represent your models in a format that is easily consumable by your clients, and make it simple to control the data that is returned in your API responses.

API resources are highly customizable, allowing you to add additional data, hide certain fields, or rename fields as needed.

API resources can also be used to handle relationships between models, making it easy to return related data in your API responses.

They also help you to keep your controllers clean and maintainable, by moving the data manipulation logic to the resources.

On the other hand, here are some potential cons of using API resources in Laravel:

API resources can add an additional layer of complexity to your application, which can make it more difficult to understand and maintain.

API resources can also be slow, especially when handling large amounts of data, as they need to perform data transformations on each item before returning it.

The use of API resources can also make it more difficult to test your application, as it adds another layer of logic that needs to be accounted for in your tests.

Additionally, depending on the complexity of your application, it may not be necessary to use API resources at all, as it can add unnecessary complexity.

In conclusion, whether or not to use API resources in Laravel is a decision that ultimately depends on the specific needs of your application. While they can be a great tool for building APIs, they also come with their own set of pros and cons. It's important to weigh the pros and cons of using API resources and consider whether they are the right choice for your application. If you do decide to use them, make sure to consider their performance, maintainability, and testability.

ABOUT THE AUTHOR

Omkar Panherkar

Omkar Panherkar is a serial entrepreneur and the founder of ShypAssist, an ecommerce logistics platform in India. He has a passion for exploring new technologies in web development and has been using the Laravel framework for the past six years. He has also published several books on Kindle to share his knowledge with others. In addition to his work in technology, he enjoys going to the gym and discussing new ideas in the tech industry.

Newsletter : https://www.linkedin.com/build-relation/ newsletter-follow?entityUrn=6952490964527570944
Youtube: @webdevelopmentwithomi